NATIVE AME

GOVERNMENTS

FROM TRIBAL COUNCILS TO CONSTITUTIONS

BY SARAH MACHAJEWSKI

Gareth Stevens
PUBLISHING

Please visit our website, www.garethstevens.com. For a free color catalog of all our high-quality books, call toll free 1-800-542-2595 or fax 1-877-542-2596.

Library of Congress Cataloging-in-Publication Data

Names: Machajewski, Sarah, author.
Title: Native American governments : from tribal councils to constitutions / Sarah Machajewski.
Description: New York : Gareth Stevens Publishing, 2018. | Series: Native American cultures | Includes biographical references and index.
Identifiers: LCCN 2017029012| ISBN 9781538208847 (pbk.) | ISBN 9781538208854 (6 pack) | ISBN 9781538208861 (library bound)
Subjects: LCSH: Indians of North America–Politics and government–Juvenile literature. | Indians of North America–Kings and rulers–Juvenile literature.
Classification: LCC E98.T77 M23 2018 | DDC 970.004/97–dc23
LC record available at https://lccn.loc.gov/2017029012

First Edition

Published in 2018 by
Gareth Stevens Publishing
111 East 14th Street, Suite 349
New York, NY 10003

Copyright © 2018 Gareth Stevens Publishing

Designer: Sarah Liddell
Editor: Therese Shea

Photo credits: Cover, p. 1 (main image) Jay Inslee/Flickr.com; cover, p. 1 (photograph) Buyenlarge/Contributor/Archive Photos/Getty Images; cover, p. 1 (talking stick) Werner Forman/Contributor/Universal Images Group/Getty Images; p. 5 Kevin Fleming/Corbis/VCG/Corbis Documentary/Getty Images; p. 7 Ævar Arnfjörð Bjarmason/Wikimedia Commons; p. 9 Scewing/Wikimedia Commons; pp. 10, 20 photo courtesy of Library of Congress; pp. 11, 21 Bettman/Contributor/Bettman/Getty Images; p.13 (wampum belt) Ineuw/Wikimedia Commons; p. 13 (flag) Marilyn Angel Wynn/Nativestock/Getty Images; p. 15 Chip Somodevilla/Staff/Getty Images News/Getty Images; p. 17 US National Archives bot/Wikimedia Commons; p. 19 Historical/Contributor/Corbis Historical/Getty Images; p. 19 Elisa.rolle/Wikimedia Commons; p. 23 JIM WATSON/Staff/AFP/Getty Images; p. 25 Bill Johnson/Contributor/Denver Post/Getty Images; p. 27 Ansgar Walk/Wikimedia Commons.

Printed in the United States of America

CPSIA compliance information: Batch #CW18GS: For further information contact Gareth Stevens, New York, New York at 1-800-542-2595.

CONTENTS

Words in the glossary appear in **bold** type the first time they are used in the text.

THE FIRST AMERICANS

When Europeans arrived in North America, they met people of different **cultures**. From their languages to their ways of life, native peoples didn't seem much like Europeans.

However, Europeans learned that Native Americans lived in societies with **traditions**, laws, and governing bodies. At first, the US government recognized many native groups as independent nations. Later, countless Native Americans were pushed from their lands to make way for settlers. They had to rebuild their communities and fight to have their governments recognized once more.

Navajo meet in the Navajo Nation Council Chambers in Arizona. Representatives of the 110 Navajo Nation chapters, or communities, speak both English and the Navajo language.

DID YOU KNOW?

According to the US Bureau of Indian Affairs, Native Americans can have several kinds of citizenship. They're citizens of the United States and of the state in which they live. They may also be citizens of a native community, sometimes called a tribe.

5

THE HISTORY OF NATIVE PEOPLES

Native Americans are indigenous (ihn-DIH-juh-nuhs) to North America. That means they were the first to live there. However, it's widely believed that their **ancestors** came to North America more than 13,000 years ago.

Modern humans first **developed** in Africa. They spread from there across Europe and Asia. They reached central Asia and Siberia about 40,000 years ago. From there, they likely crossed into North America. Over thousands of years, groups of native peoples moved and settled around the Americas.

Historians think ancestors of Native Americans crossed into North America from the area that's now Siberia in Russia (left) using a land bridge. Today, this area is covered by water.

SIBERIA

LAND BRIDGE

ALASKA

SEPARATE CULTURES

Many native cultures lost contact with each other as they moved. Thousands of separate cultures developed, each with their own ways of life. Communities needed leadership, which meant the rise of governments.

Traditional native governments differed among cultures. Many had councils of elected leaders. Sometimes elders—the respected older people of the community—appointed chiefs. Some chiefs were born into the position. Often native governments weren't official, but they still had an important role. They made decisions and established rules that people followed.

SITTING BULL

Native Americans have needed great leaders to guide them through hard times. The Hunkpapa Sioux Indian chief Sitting Bull tried to keep US settlers from taking over native lands in the late 1800s.

SOVEREIGN NATIONS

Today, there are more than 550 "federally recognized tribes" in the United States. That means the US government accepts the groups as nations with rights. These native nations are sovereign, or independent. Their governments make laws, control business decisions, and deal with other governments.

Most native groups are led by a tribal council and a constitution, or a system of governing laws. Some elected native leaders take the title of chairperson, chief, president, or governor. Native governments often include court systems with appointed or elected judges, too.

A TALKING STICK, HELD BY COUNCIL SPEAKERS IN MANY NATIVE AMERICAN TRADITIONS

Representatives from the Confederated Salish and Kootenai Tribes of the Flathead Nation meet with US Secretary of the Interior Harold Ickes, who approved their written constitution following the Indian Reorganization Act.

DID YOU KNOW?

The Indian Reorganization Act of 1934 increased Native American self-government and decreased US control. It also returned lands to some native groups.

THE SIX NATIONS

The Haudenosaunee (hoh-dee-nuh-SHOH-nee) people are known for having America's earliest **democracy**. They formed an **alliance** of nations, called a confederacy, perhaps as early as 1142. It was first made up of representatives from five nations: the Seneca, Mohawk, Oneida, Onondaga, and Cayuga. The Tuscarora nation joined them in 1722.

The Haudenosaunee Confederacy, also called the Six Nations, was led by the Grand Council, which was made up of 50 chiefs. Everyone had a vote, but all 50 chiefs had to vote the same way to make decisions.

DID YOU KNOW?

Sometimes, the people of the Six Nations are called "Iroquois." However, they prefer "Haudenosaunee," which means "people of the longhouse."

Wampum belts, made of tiny shells, record Haudenosaunee laws, traditions, and history. The design on the Hiawatha belt (shown here) represents the formation of the Haudenosaunee Confederacy. Today, the group uses the same design on their flag.

13

HAUDENOSAUNEE TODAY

Today, the Grand Council of the Haudenosaunee Confederacy is still a working government. It settles arguments and makes decisions to benefit the whole alliance. These decisions must agree with the Great Law of Peace, which is the Haudenosaunee Confederacy's constitution.

Among other points, the Great Law of Peace states that all Haudenosaunee people have rights and that their leaders are meant to serve. Many historians think the writers of the US Constitution used ideas found in the Great Law of Peace.

DID YOU KNOW?

Female Haudenosaunee leaders called clan mothers choose the chiefs who sit on the Grand Council. They can also remove the chiefs from power.

Representatives from the Onondaga, one of the nations of the Haudenosaunee Confederacy, attend a conference in Washington, DC, to speak out about issues affecting their people.

THE SHOSHONE

The Shoshone were located in California, Montana, Nevada, Utah, Wyoming, and Idaho. They were never **united** under a single government. Some bands were led by a chief, or *daigwahni*, who controlled when the community moved or hunted. Others were governed by councils of family leaders and warriors.

Today, most Shoshone groups are led by a council elected by the people and guided by a constitution. For example, the Fort Hall Business Council governs the Shoshone-Bannock of Idaho. The Shoshone-Paiute of Idaho and Nevada are overseen by the Shoshone-Paiute Business Council.

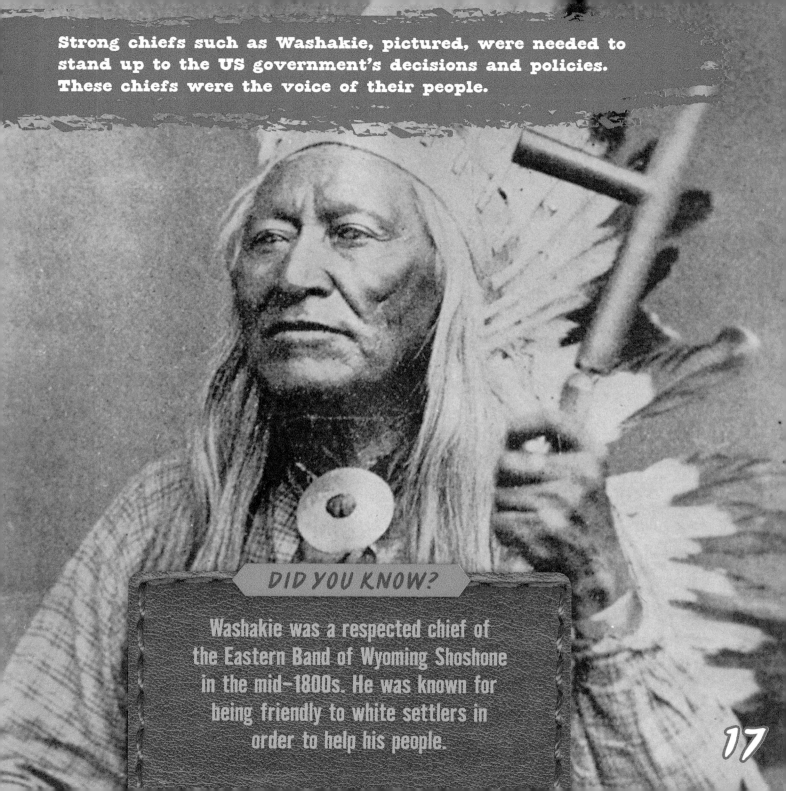

Strong chiefs such as Washakie, pictured, were needed to stand up to the US government's decisions and policies. These chiefs were the voice of their people.

DID YOU KNOW?

Washakie was a respected chief of the Eastern Band of Wyoming Shoshone in the mid-1800s. He was known for being friendly to white settlers in order to help his people.

THE PUEBLO PEOPLES

The Pueblo cultures of Arizona and New Mexico include the Hopi, Zuni, and Taos people. Long ago, Pueblo villages were independent and governed by **religious** councils. Each clan, or family group, sent a representative to the council. The council met in kivas, which were rooms built under the ground.

Today, tribal councils still lead many Pueblo communities. Twenty Pueblo governors meet for the All Indian Pueblo Council, which traces its roots to 1598. The organization oversees the Santa Fe Indian School and a Pueblo cultural center.

DID YOU KNOW?

Many Pueblo groups today don't have a written constitution. Instead, they follow traditional laws of the past.

In this photo, which was taken around 1873, leaders of the Zuni appear in traditional dress.

TAOS PUEBLO
IN NEW MEXICO

19

THE CHEROKEE

The Cherokee are native to the American Southeast. Each Cherokee town had a council house in which important decisions were made by all adults in the community, including women. As settlers moved onto their lands, the Cherokee hoped they'd be allowed to remain if they adopted practices of the white culture, including a written constitution. Most were still forced to relocate.

The Cherokee Nation is the largest federally recognized tribe today, with more than 320,000 members. Its government is made up of three branches, including a chief, council, and courts.

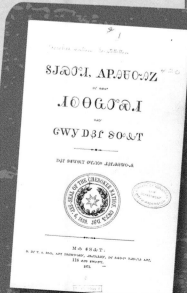

CHEROKEE CONSTITUTION

Wilma Mankiller was the first woman to serve as the principal chief of the Cherokee Nation. She was a popular leader who worked to improve conditions for the Cherokee people.

WILMA MANKILLER

DID YOU KNOW?

There are three federally recognized tribes of Cherokee: the Cherokee Nation of Oklahoma, the United Keetoowah Band in Oklahoma, and the Eastern Band of Cherokee Indians in North Carolina.

THE PLAINS PEOPLES

The Native Americans of the Plains include many peoples, such as the Pawnee, Sioux, Blackfoot, and Cheyenne. Some lived in villages led by one or more chiefs. Village chiefs met several times a year as part of a council.

Nomadic Plains peoples also had leaders. Some bands of Sioux lived in family groups called *tiyospaye* led by a headman. At least once a year, the headmen from these groups came together to decide on issues such as organizing hunts and attacking enemies.

DID YOU KNOW?

In the Plains cultures, the position of chief was often passed down within a family. However, headmen were replaced if they weren't good leaders.

Today, the Standing Rock Sioux Tribe has a constitution and a tribal council made up of a chairman and 16 councilmembers. Here, David Archambault II, chairman of the Standing Rock Sioux Tribe (third from left), sits next to President Barack Obama during an event in North Dakota.

THE UTE

The Ute of Utah, Colorado, New Mexico, and Wyoming lived in small family groups or villages. Leaders rose because of their success in war, healing, or hunting. However, they didn't have much power. Instead, decisions were made as a group. After 1934, the Ute formed governments under the Indian Reorganization Act.

Today, three different Ute groups are recognized by the US government: the Ute Indian Tribe (or Northern Ute), the Southern Ute Indian Tribe, and the Ute Mountain Ute Tribe. Each has its own constitution and council or committee.

In this 1960 photo, officials read a copy of *The Ute Bulletin*, a newspaper that covers news and topics important to the Ute people.

The Ute Bulletin

Federal Judge Ritter Temporar...
Rock Creek Range Sal...

DID YOU KNOW?

In 1986, the Utes received back
3 million acres (1.2 million ha) of land that
had been taken in the early 1900s by the
US government. This is the kind of action
that many native governments seek.

THE INUIT

The Inuit people have survived the Arctic for nearly 4,000 years. Traditionally, they lived in family communities without official governments. The Inuit began working toward building a government in the mid-1900s. They wanted control over lands and issues such as education and health care.

Many Inuit people live in a northern Canadian territory called Nunavut. The people of Nunavut elect a **legislative assembly**. The assembly then chooses a leader, called a premier, and a group of officials called a cabinet, who are responsible for running the territory's government.

The Legislative Assembly of Nunavut meets in this government building.

DID YOU KNOW?

Inuits live in Canada, Alaska, Greenland, and eastern Russia (Siberia).

27

SELF-GOVERNMENT

Strong leadership guided Native Americans long before Europeans settlers arrived. There were times in US history when the American government didn't recognize native people's right to govern themselves. They tried to separate communities and make people desert their traditions. However, the United States finally realized the importance of self-government in protecting native cultures.

No one knows the issues of the native peoples better than Native Americans. Many reservations face serious problems such as poverty and poor health care. Native governments continue to work to improve the lives of their people.

NATIVE AMERICAN GOVERNMENTS: A LOOK BACK

1400s
NATIVE PEOPLES MEET EUROPEANS FOR THE FIRST TIME. OVER HUNDREDS OF YEARS, NATIVE AMERICANS FACE PROBLEMS BROUGHT BY WHITE SETTLERS AND THEIR GOVERNMENTS.

1954
NATIVE GROUPS BEGIN TO BE BROKEN UP UNDER A "TERMINATION" PLAN PASSED BY THE US CONGRESS.

1800s
AMERICAN SETTLERS MOVE WEST, TAKING OVER NATIVE LANDS. NATIVE AMERICANS ARE FORCED TO SIGN AGREEMENTS TO GIVE UP THEIR LAND.

1970
THE US GOVERNMENT ENDS THE TERMINATION PLAN AND ALLOWS NATIVE GOVERNMENTS MORE CONTROL OVER THEIR COMMUNITIES.

1934
THE INDIAN REORGANIZATION ACT CALLS FOR THE US GOVERNMENT TO GIVE LAND BACK TO NATIVE AMERICANS. NATIVE COMMUNITIES ARE ALLOWED TO ESTABLISH OFFICIAL GOVERNMENTS.

2009
PRESIDENT BARACK OBAMA HOSTS THE WHITE HOUSE TRIBAL NATIONS SUMMIT IN WASHINGTON, DC. THE UNITED STATES PROMISES TO HONOR THE NATION-TO-NATION RELATIONSHIP AND NATIVE GROUPS.

1700s
AMERICAN COLONIAL GOVERNMENTS AND THE NEWLY ESTABLISHED UNITED STATES RECOGNIZE NATIVE GROUPS AS INDEPENDENT NATIONS.

GLOSSARY

alliance: a union between groups or people

ancestor: a person in past times who is a part of someone's family

council: a group of people who are chosen to make rules, laws, or decisions about something

culture: the beliefs and ways of life of a group of people

democracy: a form of government in which people choose leaders by voting

design: the way the parts of something are formed or arranged

develop: to grow and become more advanced

legislative assembly: a governing body

nomadic: moving from place to place instead of living in one place

religious: believing in a god or gods and following the rules of a religion

representative: someone who acts or speaks for or in support of another person or group

tradition: a way of thinking or acting that has been used by people in a group, family, or society for a long time

unite: to bring together for a common purpose or action

FOR MORE INFORMATION

BOOKS

Carew-Miller, Anna. *Native American Confederacies*. Philadelphia, PA: Mason Crest Publishing, 2014.

Hinton, KaaVonia. *The Iroquois of the Northeast*. Kennett Square, PA: Purple Toad Publishing, 2013.

McCormick, Anita Louise. *The Native American Struggle in United States History*. Berkley Heights, NJ: Enslow Publishing, 2015.

WEBSITES

Iroquois Confederacy
www.brainpop.com/socialstudies/culture/iroquoisconfederacy/
In this video, you'll learn the history of the Haudenosaunee, or Iroquois, Confederacy.

Native American Facts for Kids
www.native-languages.org/kids.htm
This site offers links about Native American history to students of all ages.

INDEX